Fragments of My Mind: A Love Letter to Anyone Who's Ever Felt Complicated, Unseen or Misunderstood

Erica Barnes

Presentation by *BookLeaf Publishing*

Web: www.bookleafpub.com

E-mail: info@bookleafpub.com

ISBN: 9789357212861

First edition 2023

DEDICATION

A Love Letter to Anyone Who's Ever Felt Complicated, Unseen or Misunderstood. You are seen. You are felt. You, are not alone.

ACKNOWLEDGEMENT

Dedicated to my beautiful babies. Da'Xia and
Isaiah, you two give me hope and purpose. I am
a better person because I am your mother.

This book is to show you, you can an do and be
anything you choose as long as you work for it
and believe God for it. Fear is an illusion, the
only one that can ever hold your back from your
greatness is you.

I love you both deeply.

-You're Mom

PREFACE

Thank you for taking a step into my world. I hope you enjoy the Fragments of My Mind.

Equipoised

She was chaos,
He, her calm.
Her mind, an alter,
To his throne.

Her body an offering,
He, her playwright.
His mind with the ability to illuminate her light.

She, his home,
His soul her host.
A rare, true love,
Fully engrossed.

The two, together equipoised, etched in time.
To never depart, forever entwined.

From this lifetime into the next.
From eternity to eternity,
Evermore effervesced.

Cemented, locked in, rooted, ensnared.
No longer single, the two, now a pair.

From two souls to one,
She his likeness, He her Sun.

You

They call me observant
That's not particularly true.
People are easy to read actually,
Especially you.

From the way you hold your coffee,
The way you look at me with ease.
To the sea of emotions you give me,
That brings me to my knees.

The sweet smiles you flash,
I can almost read your mind.
The fleeting moments that never seem to last.
Your intentions are defined.

Welcome, You're Back Home

Come Home
Deep in the depths of our subconscious our soul
is calling us back to ourselves
Come Home
Rebirth
Recenter
Recalibrate
Reignite
Realign
Remember
Rejoice, you are home
Welcome back to yourself
You are your genesis

All Along You Were Blooming

Just like the phases of the moon,
Hold space for grief, as you bloom.

One Love

One Love
Why don't you
Our love
Why won't you
True love
Why can't you
Pure love
Why shan't you
My love
Why will you
Hard love
Please don't do
Soft love
Embrace you
Wild love
I love you
Strong love
I have you
Black love
I am you
My love
Is so true

Master Me Masterfully

6

Most want my body but few want my soul,
Learn me from the inside, then out, to learn me
in whole.

Trust Me

Why are you hiding your feelings from me?
Tell me your secrets so that your soul can be
free.

Let me be the one that you can trust,
But please take your time, I'm not forcing you to
rush.

I'll be here when you need me to be,
Here's my heart, take the key.

I won't tell a soul, I take a vow,
Your secrets will never leave my lips, there's no
way how.

When you're ready to open up, let me know. I'll
hold you tight and will never let go.

You're Art

You're my congregation,
My community,
My muse,
You're my elevation,
The spark to my fuse.

Can I live in the broken pieces of you?
The boring,
The comfortable,
The convenient in you.

Can I master your hidden language,
Probe the halls of your heart.
Unveil your deep truths
You're not your brokenness, you're art

Passé

9

I would have stayed with you for an eternity
But you traded me for a fleeting moment.

There are a lot of things I can be
But what hurts the most is I could never become
yours.

Daughter Of Harvest

Daughter of harvest
You reap what you sew
Grow
Even in chaos.
Emptiness,
Confusion.
Bloom Radiantly
There is strength in your scars
You are magnificent
Gloriously magnified
Beauty personified
Virtuously certified
You are greatness verified
Wherever you go, take you're whole heart.

My Thing

Some like to dance,
Some like to sing.
I write poetry,
That's my thing.

It helps me in the worst of times,
To pour out my heart when I want to cry.

Or when I just want to be left alone,
It helps to transform me into my own.

When I'm feeling down and low,
And like there is no place to go.

Poetry is there for me,
It helps to keep me on my feet.
All I need is some paper and I'll be alright,
Through the night,
Out of sight,
Until I get my head on right.

Poetry, it is my treasure,
It gives me pleasure,
That can't be measured.

Poetry, it is my gold,
It feeds my soul,
It makes me whole.

Poetry, will never cease,
It gives me peace,
Through the agony.

Through the rain,
It eases the pain,
It keeps me sane,
Poetry, is MY thing.

We Became One

No outside interference,
No more independence,
Since we became one.

No more personal personal space,
No more time to waste,
Since our hearts became one.

No more you or I,
No more selfish lies,
Because we are now one.

No more feelings to hide,
No more reasons to cry,
Because our souls are now one.

In the Interior

In the interior,
My heart is your heart,
Your heart is mine.
Our hearts are one,
Together intertwined.

In the interior,
My soul is your soul,
Your soul is mine,
Our souls are one,
Forever intertwined.

In the interior,
My thoughts are your thoughts,
Your thoughts are mine,
Our thoughts are one,
Enmeshed, intertwined.

Daddy

Daddy Please Daddy,
Can't you hear my cries within?
The hunger for your love replaced by the lust
from other men.

Men that can never take your place,
Never fill my soul,
Never complete me,
Never make me feel whole.
Never completely, make me feel whole.

Daddy Please Daddy,
Can't you feel my pain?
The hurt of your nonexistence, driving me
insane.

Daddy Please Daddy,
Can't you feel my despair?
Your actions telling me you really don't care.

Daddy Please Daddy,
Tell me what can I do,
To make you love me as much as I love you.

Illegitimate Child

Illegitimately born.
Unwanted unowned.
Abandoned.
No place to go, nowhere to call home.
No one to hug me, hold, love me.
A misfit, dimwit, mistake, mishap.
Unscrupulous, selfish, devilish, perhaps?

These are the stereotypes placed upon me,
Is if I ask to be born illegitimately.
Why can't anyone in the world see,
Through me,
Past my illegitimacy.

We Are One

When I stare deep into your chocolate brown
eyes
Out of your soul spills your life story
Your soul takes me and shows me your world

I can hear the drumming of your heart,
So steady,
So soft,
As if it were my own.

We Are One
For that one split second,
We Are One

I can feel the warmth of your presence all
around me like a warm soft blanket

Inside it I know I'm safe there's no need to run or
hide

Flow

Let the Lord's love flow like a river's waves,
And wash away the sadness and pain.

Let the Lord's love flow to fighting nations,
And bring to them peace and salvation.

Let the Lord's love flow for eternity,
May He cover and bless us along this odyssey.

Let the Lord's love flow to everyone,
So that Christ like is what we become.

Let the Lord's love flow and bring his love and
care,
So that we can have the courage to make others
aware.

Let the Lord's love flow and wash away the hate,
God made each and every one of us for a
purpose
It was not fate.

Untitled

Beaten and torn with His head crowned with
thorns,
Still He stood tall, a human sacrifice for us all.

Not hatred but love He showed for mankind,
Because He is so righteous and divine.

Spat on and hit and torn into bits,
Lied on and betrayed, still yet He stayed.

He agreed to be slain and absorbed all our pain.
To fulfill His Fathers will,
Until He was killed.

In case you haven't realized of whom I speak,
Open your Bible and then you will seek,
Out the greatest man that ever walked the Earth,
Who is most famous for His death but also His
birth.

The King of Kings and Lord of Lord's.
He fought a mighty battle without knives or
swords.

Love and kindness seeped through His chest,

Until He took his last breath,
And His body was laid down to rest.

He shouted, "forgive them father for they know
no what they do."

Then he stretched out his arms and died for me
and you.

In My World

In MY world,
Poetry is my refuge,
My assurance
My hiding place.

Solace.

Vowels and consonants are sovereign.

Symbols that create letters, form kingdoms of
words narrating my thoughts.

Similes and metaphors are strung together
composing beautiful symphonies.

Formulating sonnets, haiku's and elfchens
Interpreting creative expressions.

My Everything

You are my everything
My in, my out
My rain, my drought
My up, my down
My smile, my frown
My sun, my snow
My depression, my glow
My winter, my fall
My one, my all

Life

Live your life to the fullest with love, hope and
meaning,
With every ounce of your being,
Never stop dreaming.

Never stop reaching towards the sky,
Keep your head held high,
And remember God is on your side.

When times get tough, life seems rough, and
prayer just seems like it's ever enough.

Remember your heavenly friend Jesus is always
there to teach us,
Free us and needs us,
To count on him when the storms are high.
When you want to smile, but you have to cry.

Just know that this too, shall pass,
And the problems that you're facing will not last.

One day soon you'll see the full moon of happier
days,
If you pray,
The Lord will take the pain away.

www.ingramcontent.com/pod-product-compliance
Lightning Source LLC
LaVergne TN
LVHW021348200726
843509LV00014B/2737